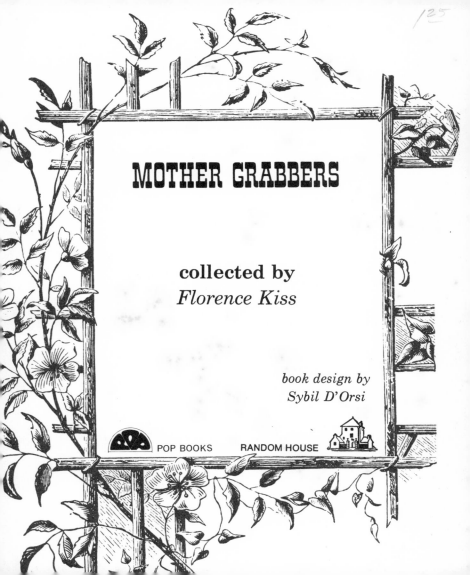

# MOTHER GRABBERS

### collected by
*Florence Kiss*

*book design by*
*Sybil D'Orsi*

POP BOOKS    RANDOM HOUSE

A POP book
Published by Montcalm Prod.,
8721 Sunset Blvd., Suite C
Hollywood, California 90069,
and by Random House, Inc.
201 East 50th Street,
New York, N.Y. 10022

Library of Congress
Catalog Card Number: 70-171210

Printed in U.S.A.

Designed by Sybil D'Orsi

*o the Mother of us all*

All I done is have him.
—*John Lennon's mother*

Honey, would you believe it? I'm a grandmother. I'm so thrilled that I'm getting a shawl to go with my miniskirt.
—*Phyllis Diller*

People's mothers always bore me to death. All women become like their mothers. That is their tragedy.
—*Oscar Wilde*

Just look at that; (she) turned them out like cookies.  —*Svetlana Alliluyeva*

Mothers' darlings make but milksop heroes.  —*Thomas Fuller*

Ah, my mother-there was a saint. Too bad!  —*Anthony Stark*

Father is writing, and mother is expurgating. *—Mark Twain*

I have been a mother to my children and I hope to be a mother to the world: ministering love, never doling it out piecemeal—but offering it in abundance. *—Dr. Louisa Duffe Booth*

My mother said
that I never should
play with the gypsies
in the wood.
If I did, she would say,
Naughty girl to disobey.
—*Nursery Rhyme*

In her new movie Bette Davis black-mails one son, exposes the second as a transvestite, drives the third son's girl into hysterics by placing a glass eye under her pillow, and threatens the life of her daughter-in-law by paying her off each time she has a baby, knowing secretly she has a heart condition.

—*Rex Reed interview with*
*Bette Davis on release of*
*"The Anniversary"*

# MY MOTHER THE CAR

—*a short-lived television show*

The hand that rocks the cradle is the
hand that rules the world.

—*William Ross Wallace*

Mothers are necessary, but so is pestilence if one is to be purged.

—*Alexandre Drey*

Old mother goose when she would wander would ride through the air on a very fine gander.

(Mom spelt backwards is Mom)

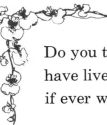

Do you think your mother and I should have lived comfortably so long together if ever we had been married?

—*John Gay*

She's somebody's mother, boys, you know, for all she's aged and poor and slow.

—*Mary Dow Brine*

I cannot bear a mother's tears. —*Virgil*

# THROW MAMA

# FROM THE TRAIN

## A KISS . . .

My mother was accursed the night she bore me, and I am faint with envy of all the dead. —*Euripides*

IS FOR

THE MILLION

THINGS

SHE GAVE ME

I gave him pot when he was younger, but now he announced he's off drugs. He keeps asking why we live in a slum. He says he wants me to wear lipstick and dresses. He's so middle class I can't believe it. Like, where have I failed?

—*Hippie mother about 10 year old son in newspaper interview.*

Most mothers don't worry about a daughter till she fails to show up for breakfast, and then it's too late.

—*Elbert Hubbard*

My mother and your mother
were out hanging clothes,
my mother gave your mother
a punch in the nose.

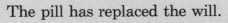

The pill has replaced the will.

                —*Dr. Arthur Franklin*

When I'm a mother—I don't want my kids to have anything I didn't have.

                —*Bertha Scheidemantel*

The fate of the child is always the work of his mother.        —*Napoleon*

Love, yes please.

Motherhood. Definitely not!

—*Catherine the Great*

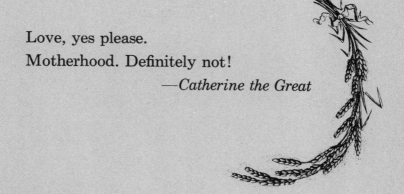

Great Mother of Pearl!  —*W. C. Fields*

JUST LIKE THE GIRL THAT MARRIED DEAR OLD . . .

I'D WALK A MILLION MILES FOR ONE OF HER SMILES

E LOVE TO SEE OUR DEAR OLD MOTHER WORK

Megaloid momworship has got com-
pletely out of hand.

—(*Philip Wylie: Generation of Vipers*)

She should have been horsewhipped.
 —*Lillian Russell*


My Mother loved me. —*Fatty Arbuckle*


Daughter am I in my mother's house
. . . but mistress in my own. —*Kipling*

Mom always liked you best.
—*Tommy Smothers*

Since Mom was a good skate, as well as a good skater, I'd take her ice-skating.
—*Ricky Nelson*


Actually mother was no good for anything except to create chaos and fear. She didn't like me because of my talent.
—*Judy Garland*


My mother always gave me enough to buy a decent lunch.      —*Ringo Starr*

YOU JUST LEAVE EVERYTHING TO MOMS.

—*Jackie (Moms) Mabley*

Oh, mother of Blue Mountain boys, come
to the screendoor, calling, "come home!
come home!"     —*Tennessee Williams*

It wasn't until I had my first physical
for the army that I learned my name
wasn't "Eddie Shut-up."     —*Ed Habib*

Behind every dead hero who lies beneath
a wooden cross over there, stands a
shining gold-star mother.

                    —*Douglas MacArthur*

The big city is like a mother's knee for many who have strayed far and found the roads rough beneath their uncertain feet. At dusk they come home and sit upon the doorstep. —*O. Henry*

There are five types of mothers which may be classified as: the supermother, the almost mother, the smothering-mother, the overwhelmed mother, and the zookeeper mother.

—*Study of the Harvard Graduate School of Education*

I would have married but I could never
find a man to match my mother.

—*Oscar Wilde*

MERICANS DEVOTE ONE DAY OF THE YEAR TO MOTHERS, AND AN ENTIRE WEEK TO PICKLES . . .

He that wipes the child's nose kisses the mother's cheek.   *—George Herbert*

Mother was unique in many ways.
      *—Elizabeth Borden*

To find out a girl's character, take her mother to lunch and get her drunk.
        *—J. Foster*

She ought never to have been a mother, but she'll make a rare mother-in-law.
        *—Samuel Butler*

BE KIND TO YOUR

WEB-FOOTED FRIENDS,

FOR A DUCK MAY

BE SOMEBODY'S

MOTHER. . . .

You have no clothes and cannot dance.
You can't go with us to the ball. We
would be quite ashamed of you.

*—Stepmother to Cinderella*

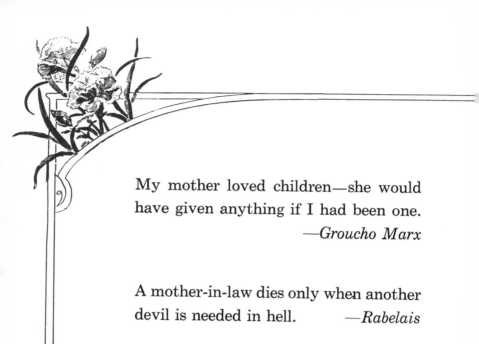

My mother loved children—she would
have given anything if I had been one.
—*Groucho Marx*

A mother-in-law dies only when another
devil is needed in hell.       —*Rabelais*

There is nothing so lonely as a mother
who is alone.       —*Irish Proverb*

I owe my mother nothin'. She never gave me a dime and I treated her likewise. —*Rosetta LaRue*

*(artist of the dance)*

DADDY,

YOU'VE BEEN

A **MOTHER**

TO ME...

Necessity is the mother of invention.
                    —*Old proverb*


In everyone's past, there lurks a mother,
sometimes two or more.    —*Cole Porter*


The mother is a matchless beast.
                    —*Scottish Proberb*


The shrill-edged shriek of a mother.
                    —*Alfred Tennyson*

OLD MOTHER
HUBBARD WENT
TO THE CUPBOARD
TO GET
HER
POOR
DOG
A BONE.

Mother's Day is a holiday celebrated by letting mother cook a bigger dinner than on any other Sunday.